ELEPHANTS ON TOUR

Published in 2018 by
Laurence King Publishing Ltd
361–373 City Road
London EC1V 1LR
United Kingdom
Tel: +44 20 7841 6900
E-mail: enquiries@laurenceking.com
www.laurenceking.com

Concept and illustrations © 2018 Guillaume Cornet

A catalog record for this book is available
from the British Library.

ISBN: 978-1-78627-222-5

Designed by Eleanor Ridsdale

Printed in China

ELEPHANTS ON TOUR

A search & find journey around the world

GUILLAUME CORNET

Laurence King Publishing

READY FOR AN ADVENTURE?

Five elephant friends are setting off on the journey of a lifetime. Packing their trunks in London, they plan to go east and travel all the way around the globe.

By joining their adventure, you will discover the secrets of some of the world's great places. Start by studying the route and meeting your new traveling companions.

SAN FRANCISCO

NYC

AMAZON JUNGLE

RIO

MEET THE ELEPHANTS

It's your job to keep an eye on the elephant adventurers.

In each place that you visit:

• find all five of the elephants

• find each elephant's favorite belonging.

Also read about each of the new places and look out for extra spotting requests from the elephants as you go!

THE EXPLORER
and his suitcase

Always ready with a plan, this elephant knows where to go and what to see. His trunk is filled with tickets and maps, and any extras can be found in his stripy souvenir suitcase.

THE FOODIE
and her cupcake

Exploring the world one delicious dish at a time, this elephant has packed her trunk with pots, pans, herbs, and spices. Hidden in her pocket is the recipe for the world's tastiest cupcakes.

THE ARTIST
and his self-portrait

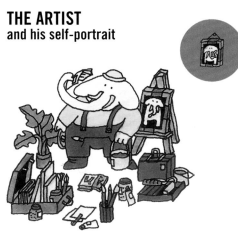

This arty elephant has always got a paintbrush or a coloring pencil ready in his trunk. Making a name for himself as an artist, he's known to hang his self-portraits anywhere and everywhere.

THE PHOTOGRAPHER
and her camera

This elephant can photograph just about anything, from sunsets and snowstorms to statues and skyscrapers. Her trusty camera is always nearby.

THE ATHLETE
and his skateboard

Always on the move, this energetic elephant can't wait to get going. His bright green skateboard is his favorite choice for high-speed fun.

First stop, London! ⟹

LONDON

Start your journey by joining your elephant friends as they ride double-decker buses and admire the river Thames.

FACT FILE

Country: United Kingdom

Currency: Pound sterling

Language: English

Population: Over 8.5 million

CAFÉ

FISH & CHIPS

THE
LONDON
EYE

SAY HELLO	Hello!
VISIT	The 25-meter-long blue whale skeleton at the Natural History Museum
DO	Explore HMS *Belfast*, a World War II warship that is now a museum
BUY	A miniature model of a red double-decker bus
EAT	A roast dinner with Yorkshire pudding

SAY HELLO	Hallo!
VISIT	Art museums to see masterpieces painted by Dutch artists Rembrandt and Vincent van Gogh
DO	Tour the city on a bicycle (there are as many bikes in Amsterdam as there are people)
BUY	Multicolored flowers from the world's only floating flower market
EAT	Stroopwafel (waffles with tasty syrup in the middle) hot from the bakery

AMSTERDAM

Ride a bicycle along Amsterdam's many cycle lanes and across its 1,200 bridges to join the elephants exploring the streets and canals.

FACT FILE

Country: The Netherlands

Currency: Euro

Language: Dutch

Population: Over 800,000

VAN GOGH MUSEUM
ONE ENTRY

ST PETERSBURG

Among the grand palaces and golden church domes of St Petersburg, the elephants can't wait to see some of the three million treasures in the Hermitage Museum.

FACT FILE

Country: Russia

Currency: Ruble

Language: Russian

Population: Over 5 million

SAY HELLO	Zdravstvuyte!
VISIT	The Mariinsky Theater to see graceful ballerinas dancing on the stage
DO	Go kayaking along the rivers and canals
BUY	A Russian doll
EAT	Blinis (Russian pancakes)

RIDING THE MONGOLIAN RAILWAY

All aboard! After making your way from St Petersburg to Moscow, you set off on one of the longest train journeys in the world. The train rumbles across Russia, over enormous bridges and through dark tunnels. The Trans-Mongolian Express then carries you down through Mongolia and the Gobi Desert and into China. From there, you can jump on a ferry to Japan.

Look out for elks!

Traditional Mongolian yurts.

Holiday highlights from St Petersburg!

THE PHOTOGRAPHER
Everyone was wrapped up warm in snowy St Petersburg. I got a great photograph of a dog wearing a brown hat with earflaps. Look back and see if you can spot him.

THE ARTIST
There were amazing buildings everywhere! Take another look and find one with a sculpture of a bird on it. That was my favorite!

Next stop, Tokyo! ⇨

THE FOODIE
I hope we can find some ice cream in the city. Keep your eyes peeled for a sign for an ice cream parlor!

THE EXPLORER
I've read in my guidebook that the transport in Tokyo is super-speedy. When we get there, see if you can spot two trains, two helicopters, and a jetpack!

THE ATHLETE
I've heard you can play all sorts of sports on top of the skyscrapers. Look out for rooftop football, rooftop basketball, and rooftop yoga.

東京
TOKYO

Join the elephants as they explore the busy streets of Tokyo, where Buddhist temples and gardens mix with skyscrapers, robots, and dazzling lights.

FACT FILE

Country: Japan

Currency: Yen

Language: Japanese

Population: Over 13 million in the main city (over 37 million in the greater area)

STAR ★ FERRY

40·18·53

FACT FILE

Country: China

Currency: Hong Kong dollar

Languages: Cantonese and English

Population: Over 7 million

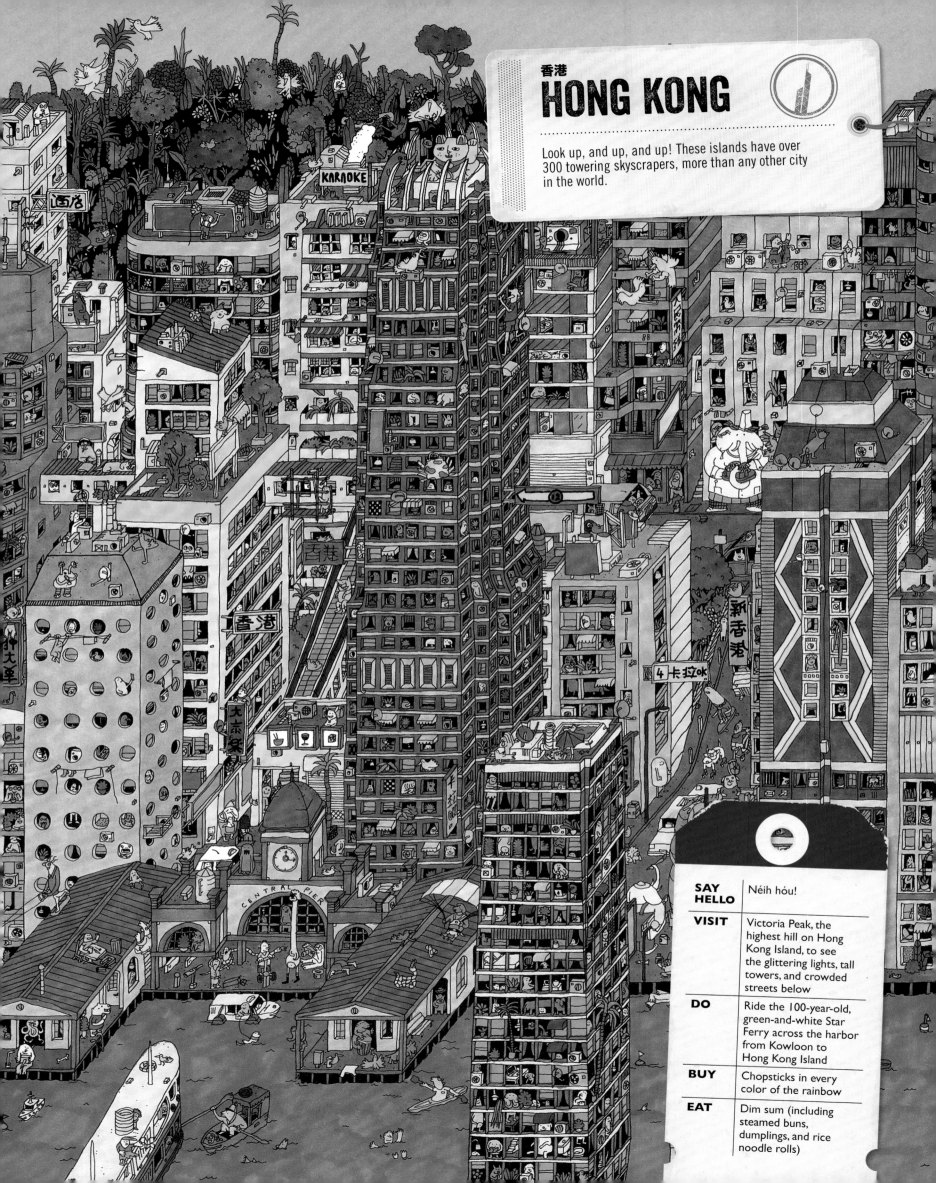

香港
HONG KONG

Look up, and up, and up! These islands have over 300 towering skyscrapers, more than any other city in the world.

SAY HELLO	Néih hóu!
VISIT	Victoria Peak, the highest hill on Hong Kong Island, to see the glittering lights, tall towers, and crowded streets below
DO	Ride the 100-year-old, green-and-white Star Ferry across the harbor from Kowloon to Hong Kong Island
BUY	Chopsticks in every color of the rainbow
EAT	Dim sum (including steamed buns, dumplings, and rice noodle rolls)

ACROSS THE AUSTRALIAN OUTBACK

The elephants find a yacht, and you sail south to the port of Darwin in northern Australia. Next, you travel more than 2,000 miles across the Outback, a vast wilderness of deserts and mountains. Camels and trucks carry you along ancient rocky tracks, on to the sunny city of Sydney.

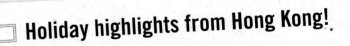

← Holiday highlights from Hong Kong!

THE FOODIE
I practiced using chopsticks every day! Take another look and see if you can spot anyone else eating with chopsticks.

THE ARTIST
I met an artist in Hong Kong and she showed me her latest painting of some flowers. Can you find it?

Animal spotting! Look out for kangaroos and birds that can't fly (called emus)!

Next stop, Sydney! ⇨

THE EXPLORER
I hope I see some kangaroos in Sydney. See if you can find one wearing roller skates!

THE ATHLETE
I can't wait to start surfing the waves. Try to find six surfboards across the city so I can meet some fellow surfers.

THE PHOTOGRAPHER
I'm looking forward to photographing the buildings, especially the Sydney Tower. It has a gold-colored observation deck and is the tallest structure in the city. Can you spot it?

SYDNEY

Climb to the top of Sydney Harbor Bridge to spot your elephant buddies exploring the harbor of a city surrounded by golden beaches and parks teeming with wildlife.

Sydney Harbor Bridge

FACT FILE

Country: Australia

Currency: Australian dollar

Language: English

Population: Over 4 million

SAY HELLO	G'day!
VISIT	Sydney Opera House, visited by over 8 million people every year
DO	Learn how to surf the waves
BUY	A koala keyring
EAT	Fresh seafood cooked on the barbecue

THE AMAZON

Crossing the Pacific Ocean takes you to South America. Canoe down the Amazon River through the world's largest rainforest, and see some of the people, animals, birds, and plants that make this their home.

AMAZON ★ **RIVER CRUISE**

FACT FILE

The Amazon is found in Brazil, Peru, Colombia, and six other countries.

Spanish, Portuguese, and over 150 tribal languages are spoken in the Amazon.

The population includes 390 billion trees, 1,300 bird species, 427 mammal species, 3,000 fish species, and millions of people.

SAY HELLO	¡Hola!
VISIT	Inca temples in Peru
DO	Avoid the flesh-eating piranhas that swim in the Amazon River
BUY	Beautiful hand-woven baskets
EAT	Ceviche (raw fish soaked in citrus juices)

FACT FILE

Country: USA

Currency: US dollar

Language: English

Population: Over 850,000

SAN FRANCISCO

Cross the Golden Gate Bridge and ride a cable car up one of San Francisco's steep hills to look down on the elephants' latest city adventures.

MUNICIPAL RAILWAY OF SAN FRANCISCO

SAY HELLO	Hi there!
VISIT	The bay to see sea lions and dolphins
DO	Take a boat trip out of the city to Alcatraz, an island surrounded by shark-infested waters that was once home to a high-security prison
BUY	Postcards from the Museum of Modern Art
EAT	Ice cream sandwiches

NEW YORK

Ride a yellow taxi through the city, gazing up at famous skyscrapers like the Chrysler Building, then hire a rowboat in leafy Central Park.

SAY HELLO	Hi!
VISIT	One of the many Broadway theaters to watch a show
DO	Climb the 354 stairs to stand in the crown of the Statue of Liberty
BUY	A New York Yankees baseball cap
EAT	Chili dogs (hot dogs topped with sauce)

BOATING
CENTRAL PARK LAKE
ONE HOUR

FACT FILE

Country: USA

Currency: US dollar

Language: English

Population: Over 8.5 million

SAY HELLO	Olá!
VISIT	The Theatro Municipal, an old theater in a building that is decorated with gold
DO	Take a cable car for spectacular views
BUY	Flip-flops to wear on Copacabana Beach
EAT	Feijoada (black bean and meat stew)

RIO DE JANEIRO

Back down to South America, just in time for the carnival! Dance your way through a city that is surrounded by mountain forests and beautiful beaches.

THEATRO MUNICIPAL

00 2340 5829

FACT FILE

Country: Brazil

Currency: Real

Language: Portuguese

Population: Over 6 million

CROSSING THE ATLANTIC

It's time for the elephant expedition to take to the skies! Fly across the Atlantic Ocean, which divides the continents of North and South America from Europe and Africa. As you soar over the endless waters, look out for some of the remotest islands in the world. When you reach the coast of Africa, carry on across to the Indian Ocean, and the enormous island of Madagascar.

Onwards and upwards!

← Holiday highlights from Rio!

THE ARTIST
The colors of the carnival were amazing! Look back and find a purple car with orange wings.

THE PHOTOGRAPHER
I got an especially good photo of an octopus wearing a top hat. See if you can spot her.

Next stop, Madagascar!

THE EXPLORER
Hopefully we'll see all sorts of animals living among the baobab trees. See if you can spot a crocodile and two flamingos.

THE ATHLETE
I've heard that the lemurs in Madagascar love sports as much as I do. Try to find a rowing lemur, a cycling lemur, and a pair of lemurs playing bat and ball.

THE FOODIE
I'm looking forward to whipping up some delicious fruit salad when we get there. See if you can spot three pineapples to help me get started.

FACT FILE

Country: Madagascar

Currency: Ariary

Languages: Malagasy and French

Population: Over 24 million (over 1 million in the capital city of Antananarivo)

SAY HELLO	Salama!
VISIT	Forests that are home to over 100 species of lemurs
DO	Walk among the baobab trees, with giant trunks that can store over 26,000 gallons of water
BUY	Patchwork cloths stitched into traditional patterns called *lamba*
EAT	Fresh fruit salad with Madagascan vanilla cream

MADAGASCAR FOREST

Don't lose the elephants among the giant baobab trees of Madagascar, which is the fourth biggest island in the world. It has thousands of animals and plants that are found nowhere else on Earth.

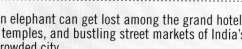

MUMBAI

Even an elephant can get lost among the grand hotels, ornate temples, and bustling street markets of India's most crowded city.

FACT FILE

Country: India

Currency: Rupee

Languages: Hindi, Marathi, and over 100 others

Population: Over 18 million

SAY HELLO	Namaste!
VISIT	The beautiful Chhatrapati Shivaji Railway Station
DO	Drink a cup of spiced chai tea
BUY	A colorful sari from a roadside market
EAT	Vada pav (potato dumpling with chutney)

CRUISING THE SUEZ CANAL

On the journey from Mumbai to Cairo, you and your elephant companions hitch a ride on some huge cargo ships coasting up the Suez Canal. It's a speedy shortcut that means ships can sail between Europe and Asia without traveling all the way round the southern tip of Africa.

Packed full of goods like oil, grain, and metal.

ERSK LINE

Wave to the camels!

Holiday highlights from Mumbai!

THE EXPLORER
I loved riding in the tuk-tuks—the little yellow and gray, three-wheeled taxis. Take another look and see if you can spot nine around the city.

THE ATHLETE
There were acrobatic monkeys all over the place. Look again and find one doing some tightrope walking.

Get comfortable — the journey can take up to 16 hours!

Next stop, Cairo! ⇨

THE FOODIE
I can't wait to get cooking. See if you can spot a spice stall in the city where I can stock up for my next tasty experiment.

THE ARTIST
I'm looking forward to seeing the beautiful minarets! See if you can spot one with a gray, pink, and yellow zigzag pattern.

THE PHOTOGRAPHER
I heard that there might be crocodiles near the river Nile. Help me spot three so I can get some good snaps!

CAIRO

Chase the elephants through Cairo's noisy streets and along the banks of the river Nile, where you can see the Great Sphinx and the Pyramids of Giza.

EGYPTIAN MUSEUM

200447

ADMIT ONE

FACT FILE

Country: Egypt

Currency: Egyptian pound

Language: Arabic

Population: Over 9 million

SAY HELLO	Marhaban!
VISIT	The Pyramids of Giza, built as tombs over 4,500 years ago
DO	See the city from the top of Cairo Tower
BUY	Paintings on papyrus (an old form of paper) from the bazaar
EAT	Koshari (rice, lentils, and macaroni, with spicy tomato sauce)

SAY HELLO	Merhaba!
VISIT	The Hagia Sophia, which was once a church, then a mosque, and is now a museum
DO	Explore the Basilica Cistern (an underground space for storing water, with a maze of over 300 columns!)
BUY	A glass lantern from the Grand Bazaar, one of the largest covered markets in the world
EAT	Baklava (sweet pastry filled with nuts and covered in syrup or honey)

ISTANBUL

Try to count all the amazing domes and minarets (thin towers with balconies) of Istanbul, a city set in two continents: stand on one side of the water and you're in Asia, then stand on the other side and you're in Europe!

HAGIA SOPHIA
ISTANBUL

FACT FILE

Country: Turkey

Currency: Lira

Language: Turkish

Population: Over 14.5 million

FACT FILE

Country: Italy

Currency: Euro

Language: Italian

Population: Over 2.5 million

ROME

In this city filled with ruins from the Roman Empire, take your elephant pals to famous churches and admire incredible paintings.

COLOSSEUM

SAY HELLO	Ciao!
VISIT	The Colosseum to imagine what it was like watching gladiators fighting
DO	Climb the Spanish Steps, which have 138 steps forming the widest stairway in Europe
BUY	Eight different flavors of gelato (ice cream)
EAT	A giant pizza!

FACT FILE

Country: France

Currency: Euro

Language: French

Population: Over 2 million

PARIS

Be the first to find the Arc de Triomphe, a stone arch that is one of this city's many monuments, and celebrate the triumph of finishing your adventure!

003 004 2184

SAY HELLO	Bonjour!
VISIT	The Louvre art gallery to see a very famous painting called the *Mona Lisa*
DO	Climb to the top of the Eiffel Tower, which has 1,665 steps (and luckily also a lift!)
BUY	Macarons from a patisserie
EAT	Croque monsieur (toasted ham and cheese sandwich)

HEADING HOME!

After jumping on a ferry and crossing the English Channel, you and the elephants arrive in the United Kingdom, back where your around-the-world journey began. Time to unpack and look at the photos!

Look back at the journey and spot these great moments. Where did the elephants see each one?

Checking out painted houses in one of America's most colorful cities.

Riding the longest outdoor covered escalator system in the world!

Admiring the minarets and domes of the Blue Mosque.

Wishing on coins at one of the world's most famous fountains.

Heading to the top of a building over 900 feet high!

Did you notice anything out of place along the way? Look again and try to find these holiday-makers.

 A London guard in Hong Kong

 An Amsterdam flower boat in Mumbai

 A Sydney kangaroo in Paris

 A Mumbai tuk-tuk in Sydney

 An ancient Roman soldier in New York

 San Francisco sea lions in Cairo

 A Rio carnival-goer in St Petersburg

 Madagascar lemurs in San Francisco

 A Cairo camel in Tokyo

 A St Petersburg local in Istanbul

 A New York taxi in London

 An Amazon jaguar in Amsterdam

And can you spot these special buildings? In which place did the elephants find each one?

 A spire with two clock faces

 An obelisk (a tall, pointy pillar)

 A decorated archway

 A bell tower

 A decorated turret

 A rooftop sheep farm

Answers for this page are circled in pink on the next page.
Painted houses = San Francisco, Outdoor escalator = Hong Kong, Blue Mosque = Istanbul, Fountain = Rome, 300m-high building = London.
Spire = Amsterdam, Obelisk = Istanbul, Archway = Rome, Bell tower = Paris, Turret = Mumbai, Sheep farm = Cairo.

ANSWERS

- ◯ = Elephants
- ◯◯ = Elephant belongings
- ◯◯ = Holiday highlights/Next stop extras
- ◯◯ = Heading home extras

London

Amsterdam

St Petersburg

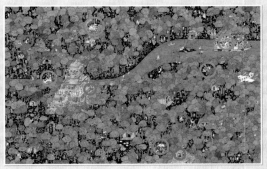
Tokyo

Hong Kong

Sydney

The Amazon

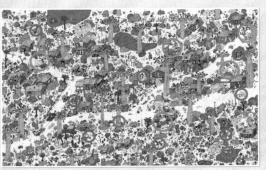
San Francisco

New York

Rio De Janeiro

Madagascar Forest

Mumbai

Cairo

Istanbul

Rome

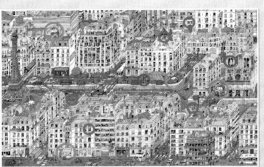
Paris

Acknowledgments

A special thank you to Cat Drew for sharing this adventure with me and always being on the lookout for those unique, bizarre moments that make life so fascinating.

Thank you to Ann Harrison and Jaccomien Klap, and to Elizabeth Jenner, Chloë Pursey, Leah Willey, and the rest of the team at Laurence King Publishing who made this possible.

Dedicated to UNIT10, a hidden place and time of my life where imagination and creativity had no limit.

THE TRAVELING ELEPHANTS!

Great Trunk Manor

Memory Lane

Tuskington North